THE MEANINGS OF MODERN ART

by JOHN RUSSELL

Art Critic, *The New York Times*

LOUIS P. GIORGI

VOLUME 2

THE EMANCIPATION OF COLOR

THE MUSEUM OF MODERN ART, NEW YORK

I. Vincent van Gogh
Bedroom at Arles, 1888
The Art Institute of Chicago

Copyright © 1974 by The Museum of Modern Art.   All rights reserved.   Library of Congress Catalog Card Number 72-76416
Series ISBN 0-87070-477-X.   Volume Two ISBN 0-87070-479-6.   Designed by Earl Tidwell
Cover: plate XIII. Henri Matisse, *Dance* (1st version), 1909. The Museum of Modern Art, New York

Between 1890 and 1905 the emancipation of color was completed.

Like most of history's upheavals, this one looks inevitable when surveyed from a safe distance. Emancipation had been in the air for a long time: you couldn't open a newspaper, sit through a play by George Bernard Shaw or put your nose inside a factory without realizing that radical changes—some peaceful, some not—were on the way. The 1860s had provided the Grand Design: people remembered 1861 for the emancipation of the serfs in Russia, 1863 for the emancipation of the slaves in the United States, 1867 for the emancipation of the Jews—in principle, at any rate—throughout the Austro-Hungarian Empire. The emancipation of women would take longer, but by the late 1880s it had become clear that society was moving toward it. It was unthinkable that in art, that most sensitive area of life, equivalent emancipations should not occur.

And occur they did, though not quite fast enough to save Pissarro and Monet from near-martyrdom by poverty in the late 1860s. Gradually it became clear that the traditional patronage of the state and the church was giving way to a freer and more informal relationship between the painter, his dealer, and just one or two informed collectors. The tyranny of the big annual official exhibition loosened around the same time, and a new tradition began: that of the little back room to which the fortunate few were admitted by pioneer dealers like Ambroise Vollard and le père Tanguy. Subject matter was set free, now that the favor of a frock-coated official was no longer essential to an artist's advancement. The fine arts were released from obligations to society which could better be carried out by photography; as a result, their natures could be explored without either inhibition or surveillance.

In all this, color was the conspicuous element. Its emancipation was foreshadowed as early as 1885, when van Gogh put it in writing that "color expresses something by itself." That color could send coded messages in a cipher not yet cracked was clear to Gauguin by 1888 and quickly got through to his disciples. That color could make volume and define form was being proved by Cézanne all through the 1880s and 1890s. That patches of color laid flat on the canvas were the prime constituent of painting, and should take rank as such, was argued by Maurice Denis, then just 20 years old, in a now-classic article, "A Definition of Neo-Traditionism," first published in August, 1890. The more men looked into the fundamentals of art, the more consistently did color turn up at the center of their inquiries.

But when color finally came out strongly at the Salon d'Automne of 1905—in the room given over to Henri Matisse, André Derain, Maurice Vlaminck, Albert Marquet, Henri-Charles Manguin and others—people were dumbfounded, all the same. They were dumbfounded all over again in Dresden in 1906, and in Munich in 1911, and at the Armory Show in New York in 1913. As in other departments of life, it is one thing to talk about emancipation and quite another to meet it face to face. There were local and auxiliary motives for their stupefaction: many of those who were appalled by Matisse in 1905 had never seen a Gauguin or a van Gogh and knew nothing of the historic fatality which had brought those particular Matisses into being. But there was also a general and a more rational reason to raise the alarm.

Color is a constant: one of the standards of excellence and normality by which we judge Nature, judge much that is of our own making, and judge one another. Color is also a differential: one of the things that help us to find our way about the world. We don't like to feel that either of these two main functions of color is subject to alteration. Color is fundamental to life: to call a man "colorless" is as rude as we can get without descending to particulars. Color has a hot line to instinct, and its messages take priority even over those of language: the hunter doesn't need to speak if he can point to fresh blood in the snow. Our first reaction to change in all this is one of defensive rigidity; if the traffic lights turned blue at the next intersection, a conservative driver would put the gears into neutral and sit by the side of the road.

But we also know, and our predecessors knew already in 1905, that color is one of the affirmative elements in life. Color is energy made visible. Energy in itself is not necessarily good; anyone who has been within range of a hurricane will have seen for himself that energy can be vicious and destructive. But in the context of art, heightened color usually brings heightened energy of a euphoric sort; and I don't think it was an accident that Matisse in 1905 was painting in a world that wanted to get more out of life than people had been getting before. What was the message of Henry James in The Ambassadors, first published just two years before? "Live all you can—it's a mistake not to."

Heightened color came into art at just the time when heightened energy of an environmental kind was becoming available to everyone. This is not to say that there was a self-evident relationship between science and art from the 1880s onward. Gauguin in Pont-Aven and van Gogh in Arles were about as innocent of up-to-date scientific knowledge as intelligent human beings can be. But they knew that there was more to color than had yet been got out of it, and that somewhere in color there was energy, waiting to be released. Color had to be made to work for everyone as electricity was working for Edison, as the gasoline engine

1. Henri Matisse
The Dessert, 1897
Private collection, Paris

was working for Gottlieb Daimler, and as Niagara Falls was beginning to work for those who knew how to tame it. These things had to have their equivalent in art; and Gauguin knew before he died that he had opened new color options for painting, just as van Gogh knew that the great artist of this century would be a colorist of a kind never seen before.

Matisse, as much as anyone, was that colorist. By 1909, when he painted the first version of his *Dance* (pl. XIII), he was able to make a plain, bald, unhesitating affirmation of color-as-energy. *Dance* looked (and still looks) so spontaneous that many people believed that Matisse had simply trusted to instinct and let rip, like a "great artist" in a movie. When Matisse opened a private art school in Paris in 1908, his students thought to please him on the first day of the term by daubing their canvases at random with the hottest colors they could lay their hands on—only to find that

Matisse disliked this very much indeed and sent them right back to the formal beginnings of art education. For Matisse knew that color, like dynamite, must be in hands that can control it.

He also knew that the Old Masters were neither ignorant nor timid when it came to the use of color. Everyone has heard of Titian's way with red, Veronese's way with green and Vermeer's way with a lapislike blue. But the conditions of art in their day were such that color had to stay down in the kitchen as the servant of form and the henchman of design.

There was even a socio-philosophical prejudice against color. Immanuel Kant, in his *Critique of Judgment*, first published in 1790, gave classic expression to the subjection of color. "In painting and sculpture," he said, "the *design* is the essential thing. . . . The colors which give brilliance to the sketch are part of its charm and they may, in their own way, give an added liveliness

4

to what we are looking at. But they can never, in themselves, make it beautiful." This was, admittedly, a philosophical position rather than the view of a man who had spent much of his life looking at pictures. Kant had hardly ever left his native city of Königsberg and was so indifferent to the pleasures of sight that it was several years before he even noticed that he had gone blind in one eye. Kant was predominantly cerebral in his orientation, and he ran true to psychological type in preferring line to color; the sensitory freedom for which color stood was of no interest to him. But, quite independently of this innate predisposition, he spoke for educated European opinion at a time when color was very much regarded as a dispensable additive; and Matisse could almost have had Kant in mind when in 1945 he looked back, as a man in his late 70s, on the evolution of color.

"The whole history of color," Matisse said then, "lies in the recapture of its powers of expression. For centuries it was no more than the complementary of drawing. Raphael, Dürer and Mantegna were like all the painters of the Renaissance in that they built their pictures on drawings and added the local color later. The case was quite different with the Italian primitives and with the painters of the Orient. With *them*, color was the principal means of expression. . . . From Delacroix to van Gogh (and, in particular, to Gauguin) by way of the Impressionists, who cleared the ground, and by way of Cézanne, who gave the definitive push when he showed us how to make volumes with pure color, we can trace the rehabilitation of color and the recovery of its power to work upon us directly."

Matisse, when he said that, had been painting and drawing and sculpting for over half a century. There lay before him, in his 80s, a terminal period as fruitful as any in the history of modern art. No one ever knew more about color than he. So what he has to say has great weight with us and, once again, the upheaval which he describes now looks inevitable.

But changes of this sort correspond to profound, hard-fought, hard-won changes in social attitudes. The long subjection of color stood, for instance, for a fear, or at the very least, a distrust of the instinctual life. By the 1890s Nietzsche had spread throughout Europe a contrary point of view: instinct was marked *plus* in his work, where for centuries it had been marked *minus*. When Kant wrote his *Critique of Judgment* it was with art as it was with property, and with monogamy, and with authority in all its forms: the instinctual life had to be kept down, lest anarchy should supervene. There was no such thing in the 1790s as a "pure colorist," in our modern sense; but any such person would at that time have been put on the official list of subversives, along with the seducer, the free-thinker and the democrat. If such people were

2. Henri Matisse
Carmelina, 1903
Museum of Fine Arts,
Boston

Matisse in *Carmelina* is concerned with a classical ideal of composition. The repeated rectangles in the background counterbalance the voluptuous fullness and roundness of the figure; and by including a little self-portrait in the lower left-hand corner of the mirror, Matisse not only gave the picture a heightened sense of depth but introduced a theme which was to be a lifelong favorite of his—that of the painter as eavesdropper.

not kept under control there would not be in all Europe a great house unsacked, a church without its Tree of Liberty, or a husband without horns; that was the idea.

Like most ideas, this one was thoroughly raked over in the 19th century. It wasn't altogether foolish, by the way. There really is such a thing as the demagogy of color: Hitler's use of black and red at the Nuremberg rallies soon proved that. But the 19th century's investigations into color were conducted for the most part in a liberationist spirit: the question to be answered was "Can color set men free, and if so how?" It seemed to Goethe, and to those who came after him, that the understanding of color was an important subdepartment of self-knowledge. Color might provide the grammar that was needed if we were to speak a new language and the keyboard that we needed if we were to draw new music from our life on earth. Ingres spoke for a steely and unalterable rearguard when he reiterated that "drawing is the probity of art"; but John Ruskin carried the century before him

II. Paul Gauguin
Old Women of Arles, 1888
The Art Institute of Chicago

Gauguin prepared the *Old Women of Arles* from life with great care and many separate studies for it exist. In the final painting, he adopted a strongly subjective approach and an emotional tone which has been called "caustic" and "sardonic." In other words, he dehumanized the old women, tilted the park bench until it seems on the point of rocketing out of the picture altogether, and remodeled the two tall stooks of corn in such a way that they echoed precisely the necklines of the two figures in the middle ground. The red fence in the lower right-hand corner of the painting serves to anchor a composition which otherwise flies upward like a kite in the wind; and the bush in the foreground can be read in such a way as to present a caricature of Gauguin's own features. When van Gogh painted comparable material in Arles he preserved his habitual reverence before life; Gauguin's picture is penetrated, on the contrary, by a mounting irritation both with the life of Arles and with the companionship of van Gogh. In all this color has a primordial role, it heightens feeling, confounds expectation and offers a short cut to understanding.

III. Maurice Vlaminck
The Blue House, c. 1905
The Minneapolis Institute of Arts

3. Jacques Louis David
The Oath of the Horatii, 1784
Musée du Louvre, Paris

The subject of David's painting of 1784 is the moment in Roman history at which the Horatii took the oath, in the presence of their father and of their grieving wives, to win or die for liberty. With the French Revolution only five years away, the picture had the clearest possible political intent.

4. Georges Rouault
Samson Turning the Millstone (Ordeal of Samson), 1893
Los Angeles County Museum of Art

Rouault never won the Rome Prize, but at the age of 22 he did his loyal best in this earnest and laborious Old Testament scene.

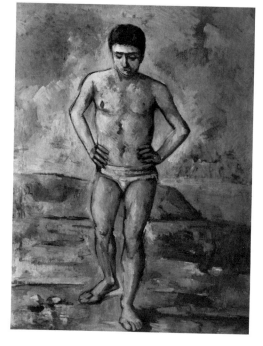

5. Paul Cézanne
The Bather, c. 1885
The Museum of Modern Art, New York

when he wrote in 1851 that "the purest and most thoughtful minds are those which love color the most."

The emancipation of color was linked, moreover, to the emancipation of art in general from social duties which had by then become obsolete. If we look at a masterpiece of Kant's day like David's *The Oath of the Horatii,* 1784 (fig. 3), we shall see at once that it carries a load of anecdote, of precise documentation and of learned pictorial references which could not be borne by the color language of 1905, even had that language been available. Interiors painted by Edouard Vuillard in the 1890s now seem to us not only ravishing in themselves but remarkably precise in their references to costume and decoration; and if, at the time they were painted, they seemed sketchy and approximate even to quite sensitive people the reason is that those people were conditioned to expect color of a tight, predictable sort. Every painting is a duet, after all. If the man who is looking at it can't keep time with the man who painted it, then the painting is incomplete; even the most radical moves in modern art have been made to an audience of not less than one.

So color was not set free in any one moment of time, as Florestan is set free in *Fidelio*. It took well over a hundred years to resolve the antithesis between the English connoisseur, Sir George Beaumont, who said, "A good picture, like a good fiddle, should be brown," and a painter like Derain, who in 1905 took a plain red, a plain blue and a plain yellow from the tube and put them straight on the canvas in rectangular dabs that subverted the whole notion of "good painting." Color was set free in a disorderly and coincidental way: by Constable when he set out to show things that "exist in Nature but have not been seen before"; by Delacroix when he noted in the 1850s that painters should "banish all earthen colors" and remember that shadows cast on the ground, by no matter what object, are violet; by Turner when he came back from his first visit to Italy and prompted Constable to say that "Turner is stark mad with ability—the picture seems to be painted with saffron and indigo"; and by Pissarro, the White Knight of Impressionism. "Such things *are*, though you mayn't believe it" was Ruskin's answer to those who could not adapt to the changing role of color in art; but there were many such people, and it took a very long time to convince them.

However, it was one of the good things about the French art scene in the 1890s that officialdom was losing its power. There were still young artists who put in for the Rome Prize, just as there were still older artists who longed for a success at the Salon. To win the Rome Prize augured lifelong success of a sedate and unadventurous kind. With this in mind, art teachers for generations had vaunted the grand formal picture for the grand formal occasion as the apotheosis toward which all studies tended; and in the 1890s Rouault, for one, did his best to comply. But for Matisse, as for Bonnard and Vuillard, the basic social relationship was more intimate. It was, in fact, the audience of not less than one: the dealer who had faith in him and showed his work to just a few people, the patron who saw him privately and not at the Salon, the like-minded friend and contemporary who fed him ideas. Those were the contacts that counted; the state could keep its medals, and its commissions for town halls and post offices, and its appointments-with-tenure at provincial schools of art.

All this favored the beginnings of modern art as a secret revolution: an experience shared initially by only a few and as often as not quite modest in format and scale. It also favored the emancipation of color, in that color is a private matter, direct in its communications and urgent in its appeal to experiences which

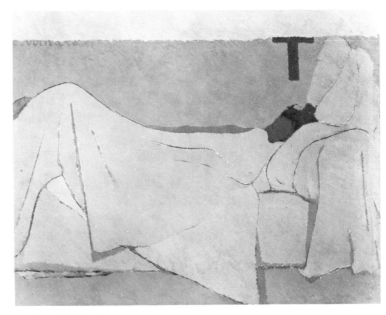

6. Edouard Vuillard
The Bed, 1891
Musée National d'Art Moderne, Paris

Painted at the height of the Art Nouveau period when curvilinear forms were being pressed into service on every possible occasion, Vuillard's *The Bed* represents a fastidious distillation of curvilinear form, steadied by the T-shape to the upper right of the painting. With a minimum of traditional modeling, Vuillard nevertheless gives us a perfectly solid, believable human being beneath perfectly believable bedclothes. The extreme tonal restraint, the witty drawing of the head, and the infectious calm of the unbroken horizontal at the top of the painting, all these are Vuillard's own, and no one else would have thought of them.

cannot always be shared with others. Color spelled out in public, as at the Salon d'Automne of 1905, was color spelled out to a disbelieving crowd. Set free in private, on the other hand, color had the fascination of a secret society: Stendhal's "happy few" were not more happy than the first patrons of Bonnard and Vuillard and Matisse.

It was by the most fortunate of dispensations that the future of French painting lay in the 1890s with very clever men. The groundwork had been done by colossal natures: people like Monet, Cézanne, van Gogh and Gauguin, who had in effect offered themselves as human sacrifices so that art should continue. Theirs were most cheerless courses, in human terms: transposed crucifixions, made bearable, insofar as they were bearable at all, by the awareness of an exceptional destiny. They enlarged our notion of human possibilities, just as *King Lear* and *Antigone* enlarged that notion. They brought to their task something more resistant, more elemental, than intelligence; but it was to intelligence, all the same, that art looked afterward. Without it, art would have foundered, no less surely than it would have foundered had not just one or two gigantic natures brought it over the hump of the 1880s.

THE MAGIC WINDOW...

What was available in the 1890s to a French painter born in 1870 or thereabouts was an idea structure exemplified by Monet, Cézanne, van Gogh and Gauguin and put into words, perhaps better than he knew, by Maurice Denis. Denis wrote in 1890 that before a painting was a portrait, a battle-piece or a Mother and Child, it was a flat surface covered with patches of color assembled in a certain order. There were two basic ideas in this remark, and both of them were important to the future of art. The first idea was that two contradictory elements had to be harmonized in picture-making: the fact of the flat surface of the canvas covered with flat patches of paint, and the fact that that flat surface was read by the public as a magic window, a window that opened, as all other windows open, onto a deep space in which everything has its allotted location. Pictorial practice hitherto had discouraged the observer from becoming conscious of the flatness of the canvas; art had been conceived as the power to make the observer—the partner in the duet—forget altogether that he is looking at a flat, vegetable object which is at most a quarter of an inch thick. If that fact was now brought home to the observer it was because color had assumed a new importance. It was also because painters had come to believe that more was to be gained by bringing that fact into the open than could be gained by concealing it.

One of the basic blunders which we can make, from our privileged point of vantage, is to suppose that the artists of 1890 knew what we know today. We have our great museums, and we have art books by the truckload, and we have tables of dates to tell us just what was happening at this moment or that; what we don't have and cannot reconstruct is the amalgam of ambition and ignorance, inner necessity and random exterior spark, which prompted certain pictures. We incline to think that a great painting is like an earthquake—something that makes itself felt at once and over a wide area—whereas it could be better likened to a murder or an act of love: a private episode, in any case, that may be discovered 20 years later or not at all.

10

7. Paul Gauguin
Still Life with Fruit, 1890
Los Angeles County Museum of Art

Matisse painted his *Oranges* (facing page) during his second visit to Morocco in 1912. He took advantage of the strong North African light to pay an incidental homage to Gauguin in his handling of the bowl of fruit. Picasso bought *Oranges* for his private collection during World War II.

We must also remember that in modern times no artist of consequence will accept a general directive. The people who imitated Gauguin were second- or third-rate painters like Charles Laval or Meyer de Haan. The people who *benefited* by Gauguin in a profound evolutionary way were the major artists who didn't paint like him at all. The last thing that Bonnard and Vuillard and Matisse wanted to do was paint portentous allegories about the destiny of mankind, as Gauguin did. Equally, it would not have occurred to them to take the symbolism of color as van Gogh took it: to see "the terrible passions of humanity" in terms of an acid red and an acid green. Life simply did not appear to them in such terms. Bonnard and Vuillard had been to schools (not art schools, but top-class general schools) at which the education offered was just about as good, and as exacting, as at any school in the Western world. When they came to make art, they made it in the image of that education. In other words, their art came out behind a shield of wit, and mischief, and elegant turn of phrase. It was not short of either feeling or sensibility, but those

IV. Henri Matisse
Oranges, 1912
Estate of Pablo Picasso

11

qualities came mostly in disguise. Bonnard and Vuillard in the 1890s had the kind of intelligent and undeceived high spirits which often follow, whether paradoxically or not, from a rigorous and demanding education. They knew what they could do and what they couldn't. Neither of them was cut out to be a preacher, like van Gogh, or to raid, like Gauguin, the mythology of peoples remote from ourselves. The life around them was their subject: whence the name of "intimist," which was given to Vuillard in particular.

An intimist is a person who studies life at close quarters. Vuillard took the life around him and broke it down in terms of flat patterns and chromatic vibrations; but he had seen a great deal of good acting and heard some of the best talkers of his day, and these two elements in his experience stayed with him when he sat down to paint. To paint was torture for Vuillard, but he never let it show: not for him the deeply-worked whirlpools of paint which mimicked the motor energies within van Gogh's nature, or the dramas of alienation behind a Tahitian sky which Gauguin sent back, batch by batch, to his friend Daniel de Monfried in France. Vuillard's dramas were of another kind: moments of social interlocking most affectionately observed and set down in an environment which owed something, beyond a doubt, to the innumerable "flats" which he had painted for his friends in the theater. He did not have to force or readjust his experience to get the flat colored areas desiderated by Denis; he had them around him in the workshop where his mother carried on her dressmaking business—in the patterned screens, in the long flat battens of patterned cloth, in the patterned papers on the long wall in the background. Matisse was later to become the supreme master of this kind of subject: the domestic interior, that is to say, in which the pull back and forth between what we see (the richly-patterned paint surface) and what the artist set out to depict is particularly rich and vivacious. But Vuillard was achieving just that, and with the utmost apparent composure, well before 1900.

Color was not, of course, the only constituent in all this. Both Vuillard and Bonnard could draw very well in a way that was peculiar to themselves: brisk, insightful, epigrammatic. They had evolved—from Japanese prints, above all—an off-center, casual-seeming form of composition that allowed them to capture the intimacies of everyday life with a freedom and a penetration which had not been brought to quite such a pitch before.

There had never, for instance, been a picture quite like Bonnard's *Man and Woman* of 1900 (fig. 8). At first glance the two figures could almost be statues niched in a wall, or butterflies framed behind glass. But at the same time they are completely and most artfully rendered in a space that is divided and made

8. Pierre Bonnard
Man and Woman, 1900
Musée National d'Art Moderne, Paris

vivid to us by the screen that rears up in the middle of the canvas and gives each figure its privacy. The two figures, both naked, bring into painting what is called in French *le naturel:* a lack of inhibition so complete that at first we barely notice it. Of course there had been bedroom scenes in painting before, but they had been of quite other kinds: gamey and equivocal, where the painter was out to titillate, or noble and generalized, if mythology was in question. Bonnard brought in a new fullness of statement and psychological grasp which made it possible for the woman to probe her big toe and the man to dry his hands on a towel without our doubting for a moment that there was an intense, ongoing sexual relationship between the two. The new candor of color, and the frank acceptance of the ambiguous nature of the painting as a physical object, made possible other candors and other forms of frankness.

MATISSE: THE INSPIRED CONSERVATIVE

Something was owed in all this to the specifically Parisian turn of mind which both Bonnard and Vuillard had perfected at school: the nimble curiosity, the belief that there was no such thing as an experience which could not be processed in terms of one more witty remark, and the Proustian sensibility which must normally be kept hooded from the world. Matisse had none of all this. He was a year younger than Vuillard and two years younger than Bonnard. During the years between 1891 and 1895, when Bonnard and Vuillard were already painting pictures which are still fundamental to the modern movement, Matisse was simply a painstaking beginner. Vuillard in his self-portraits of 1892 was an audacious colorist; Matisse at that time was still copying the Old Masters in the hope of sorting out one gray from another. Bonnard and Vuillard were in touch with the liveliest minds in Paris from their schooldays onward; Matisse got to know what had been going on in roundabout ways, or by chance. It was not until the middle of the 1890s that a painter friend introduced him to Impressionism. He was interested in Gauguin—to the point, in fact, of buying a small painting by him in 1899—but once again it was by chance that he came to see a large body of Gauguin's work when he was taken to call on Gauguin's confidant, Daniel de Monfried, in the summer of 1905.

Matisse was slow to begin, slow to get through to the great painting of the immediate past, slow to decide as to precisely what he should do about it. He had certain traits still common in northern France: he was tenacious, ruminative, almost insanely hardworking. A trained lawyer, he looked very closely at every side of a question. He had no blazing natural gift to give a decep-

9. Paul Cézanne
Three Bathers, 1879–82
Petit Palais, Paris

Matisse bought this painting from Ambroise Vollard in 1899 and kept it beside him until, in 1936, he gave it to the Musée du Petit Palais in Paris.

tive assurance to his earlier work; he had, on the contrary, a set of innate psychic checks and balances which warned him to go slow, and sometimes to stop altogether, when the moment was not ripe.

All this came out in the work. From the moment that he came into contact with the Impressionists, he could see that there was something important for him in the Impressionists' palette, which was, in musical terms, all treble and no bass. He rejected the methods in favor with the followers of Seurat on the ground that "the splitting-up of color meant the splitting-up of form and contour. The result: a jerky surface. Everything is reduced to a mere retinal sensation, and one which destroys all tranquillity of surface and contour." But before coming to this decision he made a characteristically sustained and individual attempt in the summers of 1904 and 1905 to get out of that system all that could be adapted to his own purposes.

He revered Cézanne, and in 1899 he bought a little Bathers (fig. 9) by Cézanne which he refused to sell even at times of great financial need. Already in 1900 he proved that he could model the human figure with great slabs of pure color that owed everything to Cézanne's example; but then, characteristically again, he drew back and turned to painting of quite another kind. He tested the possible modes of painting, one by one, against his own needs and his own potentialities. He even brought some of those modes to a new degree of fulfillment: his *The Dessert,* 1897 (fig. 1), is the apotheosis of the Impressionist interior, and his *Luxe,*

V. Edouard Vuillard
The Workshop (formerly *Interior at L'Etang-la-Ville*), 1893
Smith College Museum of Art, Northampton, Mass.

Calme et Volupté (1904), the apotheosis of the outdoor scene as realized by Seurat's followers. His was, as much as Gauguin's or van Gogh's, an exemplary destiny. He spoke, as they did not, for certain permanent traits of the French genius: the inspired conservatism, the power of lucid analysis, the ability to objectify. When instinct said "Drop all that and think only of yourself!" Matisse could always say "No."

Among Matisse's friends and contemporaries before 1901, none were of his own caliber. But in 1901 he happened to see Derain at an exhibition of van Gogh's work in Paris, and through Derain he met Vlaminck. Matisse had never looked young, and in the company of Derain and Vlaminck, who were extraverted giants of a generation later than his own, he must have had an almost exaggeratedly careworn and professorial look. (Derain captured something of this in the portrait of Matisse which he painted in 1905; pl. VII.) The encounter was important to Matisse because he soon found that Derain and Vlaminck had arrived at a position very similar to his own. They wanted to let color come through, in other words, without any of the constraints which the history of art had imposed upon it. Derain wanted this because he was an immensely well-educated young man who had looked at everything in the museums and decided that that was the way art had to go. Vlaminck wanted it because he was a coarse brute with just one brief spark of genius, and he wanted to prove that the art of the museums and the Salons was all washed up and could be ignored without loss. Matisse did not go along with Vlaminck in this, but he did undoubtedly derive very great comfort from the allegiance of his two juniors. (One of them wrote that Matisse "looked ten years younger" at the end of his first visit to them.)

AN AESTHETIC OF PURE EXHILARATION

Those first meetings in 1901 led eventually to what is called Fauve painting. ("Fauve" is the French word for a wild and dangerous beast.) It is in some ways a silly name, and it certainly does not suit Matisse; but it does suggest the ferocious energy with which the public as a whole was confronted, head-on, at the Salon d'Automne of 1905. (This was, by the way, the last confrontation of its kind that Paris was to see. Later developments in painting were first shown in dealers' galleries, and some were not shown at all: Picasso's *Les Demoiselles d'Avignon*, probably the most famous painting of this century, was not seen in public until 30 years after it was painted, while some of Matisse's greatest works went to Moscow before 1914 and were not seen in a French museum until 1970.)

10. André Derain
At the Suresnes Ball, 1903
The St. Louis Art Museum

Derain was a reluctant soldier, but in this very early painting he turned the irritations of army life to good advantage. A lifelong and most mischievous observer of the human comedy, he missed nothing of the awkward and yet determined way in which his colleagues-in-arms took the dance floor in full regimentals; and something of that same awkwardness came out in his manner of painting as he attempted, for perhaps the first time in his career, to combine exact social detail with a thought-out and well-knit figure composition.

Chromatic energy found in Fauvism its strongest and least ambiguous expression. An aesthetic of pure exhilaration could ask for no finer monument than Derain's Fauve landscapes. In them, a robust and for the moment undivided nature fulfills itself completely. But as Derain was a deeply intelligent man he may have sensed that only at that moment in his life, and only at that moment in the history of art, was such a fulfillment possible. For just two or three years the compass needle of painting turned toward an art that was all spontaneity, all heightened and simplified sensation. Nuance was banished, and the order of the day was "All systems go!" Derain and Vlaminck at that time disdained the gloss of "fine art": their paintings had to be seen as what they were—and for what they were.

That was never quite Matisse's position, and even Derain and Vlaminck could not maintain it for long. The rest of Derain's long career was a 40-years' attempt to recapture the qualities for which Fauvism had no place: long-pondered composition, Old-Masterly craftsmanship, learned allusion to the art of the past,

VI. André Derain
Three Trees, L'Estaque, c. 1906
Art Gallery of Ontario, Toronto

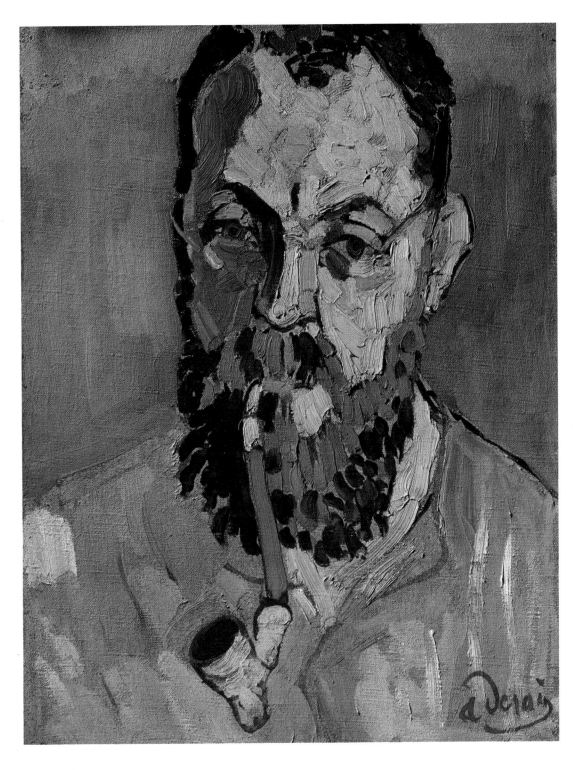

VII. André Derain
Portrait of Matisse, 1905
The Tate Gallery, London

18. Georges Braque
Landscape at L'Estaque,
1907
Private collection,
New York

19. Raoul Dufy
Sailboat at Sainte-Adresse, 1912
The Museum of Modern Art, New York

L'Estaque, near Marseilles. He had responded, just for one season, to the violent change of color and light. "But I couldn't have done it again," he went on. "I'd have had to go to the Congo the next time to get the same effect." Of course this was in part a temperamental reaction; Braque was one of the most fastidious men who ever touched a brush, and he could neither think, feel nor act to the drumbeat of pure Fauvist practice. But he adapted it, all the same, to his own nature. He brought in lavender blue as well as Prussian blue, Veronese green as well as emerald green, pink as well as vermilion, violet as well as orange. With all these, and with ivory laid on a priming of white lead, he nuanced his way across the canvas and yet stayed loyal to the Fauvist ethic: there was nothing on the canvas but the approved lozenges of unbroken color. Yet a Fauve landscape by Braque is never aggressive in the way that a landscape by Vlaminck can be aggressive; the return route to other kinds of expression is always kept open.

Braque at that time—1906—was barely 24 years old; one of the most fruitful careers in 20th-century painting had hardly begun. He was young enough and inexperienced enough not to chafe at what may now seem to us the evident shortcoming of Fauvism—the fact that it pushed color into an untenable and self-defeating position. By 1907 Fauvism for everyone except Matisse was like an army that had got ahead so far and so fast that it had run out of supplies, and run out of gas, and lost contact with headquarters. Color had been set free, but in such a way that it had nowhere to go but backward.

This was clear to Derain, who even in 1907 was reverting to forms of art in which the gamut of color was restricted in the interests of monumentality. Dufy by 1912 was working with royal blues and bottle greens and a system of tightly interlocking, Cézannesque formal units, whereas in 1906 he had concentrated on the chromatic to-and-fro of the billboards along the promenade at Trouville. Fauvism had been a sprinter's style: a 100-meter dash in which quick response and animal vigor were all-important. But great art is the province of the distance runner; and one by one, from 1907 onward, the painters worth talking about remembered this.

Matisse was the only one who never needed to backtrack or to disengage himself; he had never imagined that a progressive attitude toward color could be combined with a reactionary attitude toward other departments of art. In formal terms, the Fauve paintings of Derain and Vlaminck were conservative and unambitious by comparison with a great Gauguin. What they had to say in terms of the complexity and contradictoriness of human experience was infantile when set beside what van Gogh had had to say in Arles, in Saint-Rémy, and in Auvers. Color was given its head in Fauvist painting, but it was not free in any deeper sense, any more than a steam locomotive is set free if we take it out of its shed and put it in a meadow.

20. Raoul Dufy
*Beflagged Street,
Le Havre,* 1906
Musée National d'Art
Moderne, Paris

21. Albert Marquet
*Matisse At Work in
Manguin's Studio,*
1904–05
Musée National d'Art
Moderne, Paris

At the time Marquet painted this picture, Matisse was still very much the professional man: the qualified lawyer turned painter who sat at the easel in his city hat, his formal suit and his high white collar. By 1906 (see fig. 43) the lawyer look had fallen away and Matisse, in his striped T-shirt, was clearly someone who spent much of his time in Algeria (1905–06) and on the Mediterranean coast of France (1906–07).

22. Maurice Denis
Homage to Cézanne, 1900
Musée National d'Art Moderne, Paris

In 1901 Maurice Denis sent to the Paris Salon a painting which was, in effect, a manifesto of solidarity with Cézanne. Around a still life by Cézanne are grouped (left to right): Odilon Redon, Edouard Vuillard, Xavier Mellerio, Ambroise Vollard, Maurice Denis, Paul Sérusier, Paul Ranson, K.-X. Roussel, Pierre Bonnard and Madame Maurice Denis.

Fauvism had made a great contribution to the natural history of exuberance; but by 1907 people were beginning to look around for something less limited.

They found it in the threefold revelation of Cézanne which took place in the fall of 1907. Cézanne had died in Aix-en-Provence in October, 1906. Just a year later, what had been known to only a few was made apparent to everyone—that the new century had everything to learn from Cézanne. There was a retrospective of 48 oil paintings at the Salon d'Automne; there were 79 watercolors at the Bernheim-Jeune gallery; there was the publication in the *Mercure de France* of his letters to a young painter, Emile Bernard. Nothing was ever the same again in living art.

All this was a surprise to most people, but it was not a surprise to Matisse, who for eight years had studied his own small but masterly Cézanne hour by hour. Quite possibly it was because of the uproar around him that he agreed to set out his own ideas, once and for all, in a now-famous article called "A Painter's Notes," which came out in *La Grande Revue* in December, 1908.

VIII. André Derain
London Bridge, 1906
The Museum of Modern Art, New York

22

Like most pronouncements of its kind, this one has been pored over, and turned this way and that, and tilted to suit every imaginable purpose. But there does emerge from it, even so, a coherent picture of what Matisse was trying to do.

Matisse did not see it as the function of the painter to describe what he saw, or to confirm the teaching of conventional vision, or to record immediate sensation in a vivid and garrulous way. On the contrary: he thought of each of his paintings as an object new-born into the world. It was, in his own words, a "condensation" of experience, not an imitation of it. In earlier painting there had usually been gradations of intensity, with areas of maximum interest and focal points toward which everything in the composition tended. Meanings had been signalled in ways universally understood by what Matisse called "passions mirrored upon a human face or revealed by a violent gesture." In a Matisse there was nothing of this. Every part of the painting ranked as equal in meaning with every other part; the expression—and Matisse valued expression above all things—lay not in the thing portrayed but in the organization of the surface of the painting. The quintessentials of the act of painting were that it was considered, steady and deep; each painting was to be a portrait of human nature at one with itself.

The role of color in all this was fundamental. Color was to be full, weighty, individual and perfectly judged. Color was to be allowed to build *on its own*; it was to work on the flat, with an august personal rhythm which came from the painter's inmost nature; and it was to work in depth, building the forms, situating them in space, making them free citizens of an ideal republic of the eye. And that republic must endure: whatever was built must stand up forever.

Matisse in all this was opposing himself to everything in painting that was descriptive and pedestrian, on the one hand, or fugitive and undigested, on the other. Above all, the emancipation of color must be linked to the emancipation of all other constituents of painting; the artist must be as free to reinvent space, and to restructure form, as he was to release color. If he succeeded in all this—if he justified, among other things, the abandonment of literal representation—there might come into existence "a higher order of beauty."

After a hundred years of the "modern movement," we know that that higher order of beauty of which Matisse wrote is likely to present itself in guises unfamiliar to us. This causes us to be, if anything, overenthusiastic: to confound the novel with the new, in other words. Before 1914 this was not the case. The "audience of not less than one" was quite often reduced to an audience of not more than one; and in 1905, when Matisse's Fauve paintings

23. Henri Matisse
Reading, 1905–06
Private collection,
New York

Reading reintroduces some of the ingredients of traditional still life with which Matisse had concerned himself as a beginner: the jug, the bowl of fruit, the flowers. But the quick, nervous, broken touch and the summary indications of form forecast a complete and imminent change of method; only the figure of his daughter, bent over her book, has a traditional solidity.

went on show, the reaction of the public was so violent that Matisse had to forbid his wife to go into the gallery in question.

This hostility was directed against Matisse in large part because his new methods were applied not only to landscape and to still life but to the human face. People very much dislike the idea that the accepted look of the human face on canvas can be dismantled and discarded. Something of their own identity is at stake, whereas landscape and still life can be taken apart and restated with much less menace to the individual psyche. Matisse offended by putting a broad green stripe down the middle of his wife's forehead, by putting a bright red boundary mark where forehead gives way to hair, and by dividing the face into sharply delineated color areas; and his offense was compounded by the fact that those color areas related more to the empty spaces adjacent to the face than to any conventional idea of the unity of the human complexion (pl. X). People simply didn't realize that every part of the picture was as expressive as every other part; refusing to see this, they missed the point—which was that the painting was a tender and most recognizable likeness of an individual human being.

23

24. Henri Matisse
Jeannette IV, 1910–13
The Museum of Modern Art, New York

Matisse made in all five heads of Jeanne (Jeannette) Vaderin. The first two were modeled in traditional style, direct from life. After which Matisse felt free to edit and revise the given facts: changing the hairstyle, deepening the eyesockets, emphasizing the long crooked nose, and devising a new form of base, in which the head, neck and chest merge without modulation into an urn-like form. Body and base area are one, in *Jeannette IV*, and the sculpture is simultaneously a powerful, totemic image in its own right and a vivid likeness of an identifiable human being.

The chromatic issue was not, to Matisse's way of thinking, something that could be detached from the other considerations which govern the making of a major work of art. Nor did he think that any one color was "beautiful" or expressive on its own. What interested him was the interrelation and the interdependence of a whole group of colors. In his Fauve period he never transcribed his color literally, as his colleagues did when they chose subjects which had vivid color built into them: billboards, or a street decked out with the red, white and blue of the French national flag (fig. 20). His color was based on feeling, not on imitation; Madame Matisse is said to have posed in a black dress for some of the most brightly colored of his portraits of her.

Matisse in a quiet way was one of the most ambitious men who ever lived. His ambitions extended, moreover, to every department of art: there was not one of them that he did not intend in time to hump on his shoulders and haul bodily into a new phase of its development. To this end he would spend years on a single small sculpture, drag himself across Paris night and day from one art school to another, and ruminate on the art of the past—European, Islamic, "primitive"—as if wondering against what to measure himself next. As he was also, in terms of his work, a late developer, it came about that the great pictures which he painted in his late 30s and early 40s were quite remarkably rich, dense and various.

In this he was prompted by the ancient and honorable tradition of the masterpiece: the big-scale work into which the artist puts all he has got. Matisse in the 1890s had lived through the time when painters were haunted by the idea of the wall-sized decoration. The 19th century had been possessed throughout by the idea of the very large picture: Géricault's *The Raft of the "Méduse,"* 1818–19 (Volume 1), Delacroix's *Death of Sardanapalus* (c. 1827), Courbet's *Burial at Ornans* (1849), Monet's fragmentary *Le Déjeuner sur l'herbe*. Cézanne in his *Grandes Baigneuses* (Volume 1) carried into the 20th century the notion of the very large painting as a mark of manhood; and now someone had to take up the torch which had fallen from Cézanne's hand.

PICASSO: THE FIRST STRIKE

To an extent which we can now never define, Matisse was affected at this time by the fact that since the summer of 1904 Picasso had been living and working in Paris. Picasso himself will figure so often and so largely in this series that I need only say of him here that he too manifested, during the years in question, a most resolute intention to draw a firm black line beneath the history of painting to date and head out toward the future in which his role would be predominant. This was clear from his general deportment: in the *Self-Portrait* of 1906 (fig. 42), for instance, he holds the palette as a Greek warrior might hold his shield. It was also clear from the series of major paintings which he undertook between 1903 and 1907: *La Vie*, 1903 (fig. 32), the *Acrobat with a Ball*, 1904–05 (fig. 41), *Family of Saltimbanques*, 1905 (pl. XII), *Boy Leading a Horse*, 1905–06 (fig. 26), and above all, *Les Demoiselles d'Avignon*, 1907. Picasso was out to capture art as a great general captures a walled city: by storm.

There was no question, where Matisse and Picasso were concerned, of crude rivalry or thick-witted emulation. After Matisse died, Picasso said to a friend, "I have to paint for both of us now"; and the remark indicates to what an extent, for over half a century, the two great men were aware of one another—never

25. Pablo Picasso
Self-Portrait, 1901
Mr. and Mrs. John Hay
Whitney, New York

One of the earliest of Picasso's self-portraits, this was painted in the late spring or summer of 1901, not long after Picasso had arrived for his second stay in Paris. The driving energy of the paint structure combines with the hypnotic steadiness of the gaze to produce a most telling "portrait of the artist as a young man."

26. Pablo Picasso
Boy Leading a Horse,
1905–06
The Museum of Modern
Art, New York

In this painting, as much as in the slightly earlier *Family of Saltimbanques,* Picasso pioneered the vision of a timeless and heroic humanity, set free from all local connotations and sited against a shelving, featureless hillside, which Matisse was to perfect in *Dance* and *Music.* There is also a clear link with Cézanne's chunky, un-idealized *Bather* of c. 1885 (fig. 5).

competing, but never forgetful, either, of the colossal contribution of the other.

They were never friends, in the sense that Picasso and Braque, or Matisse and Derain, were friends at one time. There was no direct influence, of the kind that Seurat had had on Signac, or that Cézanne was to have upon a whole generation. Temperamentally, they were as distinct from one another as it is possible for two men to be. Matisse was measured in his utterance, slow and thorough in his approach to any new idea, unbending in his insistence on the privacy of the home. Picasso was direct and piratical, acquisitive and quick to take fire: no one has ever been faster to process a new idea. He was a predestined autobiographer, a confidant who kept nothing back from his public, and whereas Matisse went into his apartment as Noah went into the Ark, seeing it as a sanctuary indispensable to life, Picasso regarded his friends, male and female, as a kind of traveling repertory company which could go through its paces in the street, or at a café table, and did not need any more formal environment.

Matisse and Picasso were not so much opposites, therefore, as complementaries. When Picasso spoke of Matisse and himself as "the North Pole and the South Pole," he doubtless meant that they were a long way apart; but he also meant that they were landmarks indispensable to the map of modern art. Without them, that map would make no sense.

Picasso was not a "colorist," then or later, but he was a man who used color, as he used every other constituent of art, with a kind of ferocious sufficiency. He did not aim to reinvent the whole notion of color, but he could make color do what he wanted. From the time of his second visit to Paris in 1901 he used

IX. Kees van Dongen
Modjesko, Soprano Singer, 1908
The Museum of Modern Art, New York

Van Dongen throughout his life had a crude, hearty and quite unaffected enjoyment of whatever was oddest and most strongly individual in popular entertainment. This portrait of a female impersonator is deliberately "larger than life": more vivid, stronger in color, more monumental in pose and physique. And van Dongen in 1908 was hoisted out of his class by the company and the example of great artists; the weaknesses of his talent and of his rackety, self-indulgent nature, did not yet appear.

X. Henri Matisse
*Portrait of Mme. Matisse
with a Green Stripe,* 1905
The Royal Museum of Fine Arts,
Copenhagen

27. Pablo Picasso
The Blue Room (La Toilette), 1901
The Phillips Collection, Washington, D.C.

28. Pablo Picasso
Woman Ironing, 1904
The Solomon R.
Guggenheim Museum,
New York

color in a direct, all-over, instantly recognizable way. Color in his Blue Period paintings operates as a strong rinse that tells the observer just what is demanded of him. (The little painting called *The Blue Room* of 1901 [fig. 27], shows how well Picasso took the point of the poster by Toulouse-Lautrec which figures in it: Picasso had already learned to signal with color in the way that Lautrec used blue and yellow to signal the merits of May Milton.)

People have always reacted strongly to the paintings of Picasso's Blue Period. Blue in itself has melancholic associations for almost everyone; and the pictures combine poignancy of subject matter and a simplified emotional structure in ways which make them immediately accessible. We don't need Picasso to tell us by his choice of emphatic subject matter that it is a misfortune to have nothing to eat and an even greater misfortune to go blind. But it is possible to feel that many of these paintings are really rather mawkish. Not only is color being used, but we ourselves are being used also. Passivity before misfortune is not in itself an admirable trait, and if we compare Picasso's *Woman Ironing* of 1904 (fig. 28) with Degas's two great paintings of a similar subject, there is no doubt that with his robust, caustic, and yet deeply human handling, Degas gets much the better of the comparison.

Color in a Blue Period Picasso has too often the role of an emotional additive, wished up from nowhere to reinforce a point which is already well made in black and white work of the period.

It is hazardous to attribute, at nearly 70 years' distance, motives and reactions to one of the most combustible natures that ever existed, but it is also beyond argument that Picasso's almost preternatural intelligence had a great deal more to bite on in Paris, from the summer of 1904 onward, than it ever had in Barcelona. Barcelona, at the turn of the century, was the most stylish and cosmopolitan of Spanish cities; nowhere in Europe was there a wider, richer and more eager intake of ideas from abroad. But there is a difference between living in a place where things are talked about and living in a place where they are done; and Paris in 1904 was the place where things were being done.

What was being done in Paris was powered above all by the belief that the next great thing, in art, must follow logically from the last great thing. Inspiration had its part to play; but the best artist, other things being equal, was the one who made most sense of history. Matisse had always believed this. Picasso had known it ever since he had first been exposed to the crossbred

29. Edgar Degas
The Ironers, 1882
Norton Simon, Inc. Museum of Art, Los Angeles

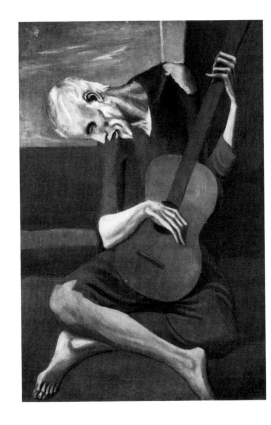

30. Pablo Picasso
The Old Guitarist, 1903
The Art Institute of
Chicago

artistic life of Barcelona; and in *La Vie* he had drawn directly on van Gogh in the hope of basing a major pictorial achievement on the art of the immediate past. But at the time when he came to live in Paris, that immediate past was being given a particular grandeur by the appearance of 42 paintings by Cézanne at the Salon d'Automne of 1904, and of smaller but still substantial groups of Cézannes at the Salons of 1905 and 1906.

COLOR AS SHELLBURST

Such things could not be digested quickly. They corresponded to a profound change in the nature of human understanding. Things looked different, in Cézanne's paintings, because they had become known to be different. Merely to ape the outward appearance of a painting by Cézanne would get nobody anywhere. It was several years before Picasso could deal comprehensively with his reactions to Cézanne; and even Matisse, who lived with a Cézanne on his own walls, had every imaginable difficulty in mastering its lessons. Meanwhile there was something exclusive, something all-devouring, about the preoccupation with what Derain called "color for color's sake." When Matisse

and Derain were together at Collioure in the summer of 1905, they were bent on going much further than anyone had been before in the direction of color which was completely dissociated from everyday associations. Here for instance is how Alfred Barr, in his pioneering book on Matisse (1951), once described a landscape painted by Matisse at Collioure that summer. The color, he said, "seems completely free of any responsibility for description of natural appearances. The tree trunks, for instance, as one reads the picture from left to right, are blue-green, maroon, bright blue, yellow-green, scarlet and purple, dark green and violet, and at the right, ultramarine. They spring from a ground that is spotted blue, orange, ochre and sea-green, and they carry foliage of vermilion, green and lavender. Only the sea in the distance and the sky retain their natural color."

Color thus used was like a shellburst on the surface of the canvas. Only after a while did the observer learn to read the forms, and read the space; and only if he was very bright indeed would he realize that in this Matisse landscape he was looking at an unpopulated variant of a subject that had been in and out of European art for hundreds of years: the Golden Age.

XI. Henri Matisse
Open Window, Collioure, 1905
Mr. and Mrs. John Hay Whitney,
New York

30

31. (*above*) Pablo Picasso
The Frugal Repast, 1904
The Museum of Modern Art, New York

32. (*left*) Pablo Picasso
La Vie, 1903
The Cleveland Museum of Art

This work has echoes of Puvis de Chavannes—in the ivory-like flesh, the stylization of the poses and the broody, dream-haunted character of the image as a whole. But in his first full-scale attempt to sum up "the meaning of life" Picasso also drew on van Gogh, who at that time had a great influence upon him. For example, the crouching figure portrayed in the lower half of the canvas derives directly from van Gogh's *Sorrow* of 1882. Picasso's exact intentions in *La Vie* remains enigmatic; but the plight of the young lovers at odds with life and with the instinctual forces which surround them was common ground for many gifted painters at the turn of the century.

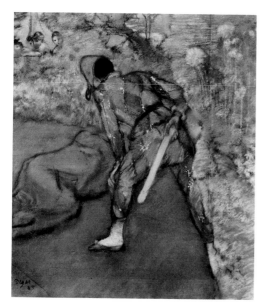

39. Edgar Degas
Harlequin, 1885
The Art Institute of
Chicago

Degas was, for all his life, a connoisseur of popular entertainment; in this instance he was 20 years ahead of Picasso in his understanding of the brief, mysterious authority which costume confers.

40. Pablo Picasso
*Two Acrobats with a
Dog*, 1905
The Museum of
Modern Art,
New York

Golden Age—stilted as it may be—and they would see that the two paintings are closely allied in their readiness to violate academic anatomy in the interests of a broad, flowing arabesque set against a heavily wooded landscape that was cut open in the center to give depth and admit of a far blue distance.

The *Joy of Life* hung for years in Gertrude Stein's drawing room in Paris, where Picasso was a frequent visitor. He must, consciously or not, have seen the big picture as a challenge to his own capacities; and when he came to paint the *Demoiselles d'Avignon* he began from a compositional scheme which was strikingly akin to that of the *Joy of Life*. *Les Demoiselles d'Avignon* will dominate a later chapter in this account to such an extent that I need say here only that, like the *Joy of Life*, it has to do with grouped human figures set in a tripartite formal design that varies in color from warmth on the left to a cooler, sharper climate on the right. Again like the *Joy of Life*, though in a way that is altogether more trenchant, it treats the individual figures in a variety of styles, with no attempt at internal consistency.

PORTRAITS OF DISCONNECTION

Meanwhile Picasso, in his 25th year, was working on two monumental projects which had in common an instantly identifiable pinkish tonality. Picasso's Rose Period would seem to have begun in March, 1905, with a painting in gouache and watercolor of a young acrobat. Thereafter he produced a substantial corpus of paintings and drawings of circus- and street-performers, in costume and out of it. Their general subject was the contrast between the beauty and fragility of the human body and the feats of strength and endurance which it can be trained to carry out. With this came a subsidiary contrast: between the enclosed world of the performers and the world which we ourselves inhabit. The poet Rainer Maria Rilke knew Picasso's *Family of Saltimbanques* very well, and he wrote about it in one of his "Duino Elegies." He saw the little family as having been tormented from childhood onward by the will toward a brief, hard-won perfection: a fugitive beauty which few would notice and fewer still would stay to applaud. The *Family of Saltimbanques* was intended in this sense, beyond a doubt; but it is also a metaphor for the painter's position in society.

Picasso in the *Saltimbanques*, and in the never-finished project of 1906 for a large painting of horses and their attendants, was carrying forward a tradition in which Manet, in particular, had excelled: that of the complex figure composition in which people, often costumed beyond the demands of everyday, were grouped in an informal manner. The paintings in question can be

XII. Pablo Picasso
Family of Saltimbanques, 1905
National Gallery of Art, Washington, D.C.

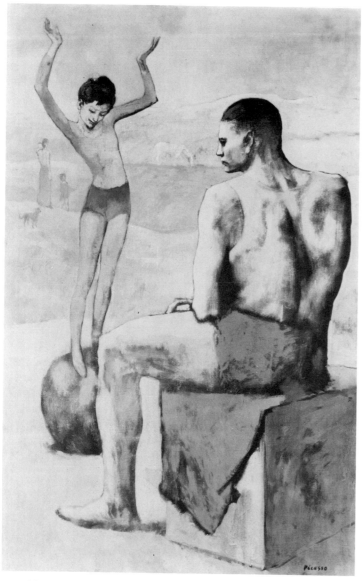

41. Pablo Picasso
Acrobat with a Ball, 1905
Pushkin Museum, Moscow

Picasso, in pre-Cubist days, was a master of the symbolic subject that evokes, but does not emphasize, some permanent aspect of the human predicament. In this painting he contrasted the slender, androgynous body of the young acrobat, so precariously balanced on the ball, with the inert and colossal bulk of the older performer, so heavily, wearily, immovably set down on his rectangular perch. Innocence and experience, fragility and more-than-human strength, ball and cube—each finds its opposite in one of the most moving of Picasso's earlier images.

42. Pablo Picasso
Self-Portrait, 1906
Philadelphia Museum of Art

read as portraits of disconnection, though there is no reason to think that Manet (or Watteau before him, in his theatrical paintings) so intended them. "Alienation" is, even so, our current name for the look of apartness which Manet gives to the old musician and his companions (fig. 47); and it recurs in Picasso's *Family of Saltimbanques.* Color in the big Picasso defines the emotional climate of the picture—and how subtly! Those faded pinks and subdued terra cottas, those echoing blues are picked up by the colors of earth and sky; the flowers in the child's basket index them all over again; even the pitcher on the ground plays along.

43. Henri Matisse
Self-Portrait, 1906
The Royal Museum of Fine Arts, Copenhagen

44. Pablo Picasso
Horses at the Watering Place, 1906
Worcester Art Museum, Worcester, Mass.

45. Pablo Picasso
Figures in Pink (The Harem), c. 1905–06
The Cleveland Museum of Art

In 1906 Picasso was feeling his way toward the complex figures-in-an-interior theme which found uniquely powerful expression a year later in the *Demoiselles d'Avignon*. *Figures in Pink* is a transitional, unresolved painting in which echoes of earlier painting (Ingres's *Venus Anadyomene*, for instance, in the standing figure on the left) are combined with certain current preoccupations of Picasso's own—the reclining giant in the right-hand corner, for one. The theme of captive womanhood never ceased to fascinate Picasso, and in the 1960s he produced a long series of variations on another classic in the genre—Delacroix's *The Women of Algiers*.

We would suppose that all this was as much a product of Picasso's imagination as the recurrent washes of moon blue in his paintings of a year or two earlier. But it has been pointed out that some of the Rose Period paintings deal—in terms of straightforward local color—with the facts of life among circus performers.

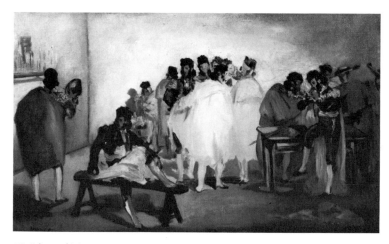

46. Edouard Manet
Toreadors at Rest (La Posada), c. 1865
Hill-Stead Museum, Farmington, Conn.

47. Edouard Manet
The Old Musician, 1862
National Gallery of Art, Washington, D.C.

It was a matter of literal truth that the interior of the most popular circus in Paris was painted "a tender red, shading slightly into gray," and that acrobats traditionally wore what one writer called "pink tights tinted the color of fresh roses." Indeed, Degas and Seurat had treated that same circus building in tones of rose, pink and red. There is therefore no reason to think of the color in these paintings as a bid to preëmpt our sympathies. Touching as it is, it remains primarily descriptive.

The delectable paintings of circus performers which figure so largely in Picasso's Rose Period were linked to life, therefore, by their use of color which was, in effect, a mark ·of professional identification: circus pink was as specific, in this context, as "navy blue." But the Rose Period also corresponded to a basic change of mood in Picasso's output; and that change of mood persisted in the more directly autobiographical work of the period—the self-portraits, the affectionate variations on the looks of his best friends, and the sideway allusions to the role of the artist in society. Matisse was altogether more detached—more cool-hearted, many would say—in his choice of subject matter. And whereas Picasso could manipulate circumstantial detail to most poignant effect, Matisse tended between 1905 and 1910 to eliminate more and more all those elements in his figure paintings which could detract from the central role of color.

When Matisse's Russian patron Shchukin asked him, for instance, for a decorative panel on the theme of music, he began with a sketch which showed people in the standard attitude of enraptured concertgoers; standard flowers grew at their feet, and a standard mastiff completed the scene. But before long he cut out the flowers, cut out the dog, cut out the self-awareness of the listeners. Color had been set free, and now it must be *left* free: that was the message of the two big decorations, *Dance* and *Music* (fig. 48), which Matisse sent to Moscow.

COLOR AS ENVIRONMENT

The Museum of Modern Art possesses the first version (1909) of *Dance*. From the study of this, and more particularly from the study of *The Red Studio* of 1911 (pl. XIV), we can see exactly what "color for color's sake" could mean at that time. It meant—as Matisse told his students—building the picture in terms of color. It meant getting the colors to support one another without anecdotal references or any resorting to "local color." Nature must be made to submit to "the spirit of the picture"; and that spirit was to be expressed in terms of pure color, as intense as the painter could make it. Color must do all the talking.

Matisse decided to build *Dance* with three colors: in his own

XIII. Henri Matisse
Dance (1st version), 1909
The Museum of Modern Art, New York

48. Henri Matisse
Music, 1910
The Hermitage, Leningrad

words "a beautiful blue for the sky, the bluest of blues (the surface was colored to saturation, that is to say, up to a point where the blue, the idea of absolute blue, appeared conclusively) and a like green for the earth, and the vibrant vermilion for the bodies." Matisse had experimented with maximum saturation the year before with a single bathing figure. Now he took a group of dancers from the middle ground of the *Joy of Life* and brought them up front, on the kind of anonymous promontory that Picasso had used for his *Family of Saltimbanques*. The Museum of Modern Art's version has not quite the chromatic intensity of the Moscow version, and some of the drawing is more felt than realized: the detailing of hands and feet, for instance. The New York painting is about an uncomplicated form of high spirits; the Moscow one, about what could almost be a dance to the death, such as was to be portrayed in the music of Stravinsky's *The Rite of Spring*. But the two big paintings should be contrasted rather with the classic

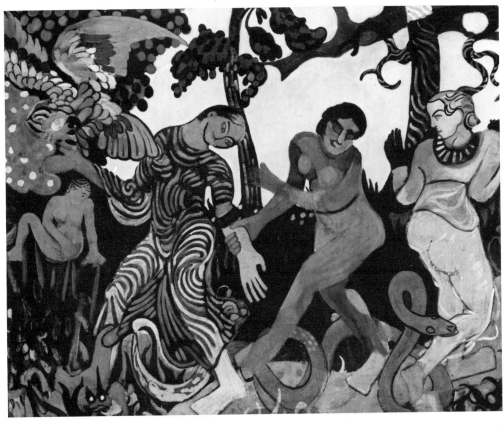

50. André Derain
The Dance, 1905–06
Fridart Foundation, Geneva

Derain as a young man was insatiably ambitious and would settle for nothing less than mastery of all the standard genres of European painting: landscape, still life, portraiture and the full-scale figure subject. He attempted this last in *The Golden Age*, and he attempted it again in *The Dance*, which predated Matisse's great treatment of the subject by nearly four years. The picture cannot be called a success; but there is a very strong period flavor about the frieze-like presentation of the dancing figures, and their portrayal in flattened outline against what could be a drop-curtain for the theater. It should surprise no one who has seen *The Dance* that Derain later became one of the liveliest and most inventive of stage designers.

bacchanalia of European painting than with one another. Poussin's *Bacchanalian Scene*, 1636–37 (fig. 49), has, for instance, a comparable round dance, with comparable positioning of hands and feet and a comparable circular pounding swing, round and round, as if naked figures had picked up Energy itself, as one might pick up a ball, and were flinging it from hand to hand. But Poussin upholstered the image with allegorical by-play in ways which Matisse by 1909 felt free to discard; in *Dance* there are no garlanded satyrs, no overhanging foliage, no distant mountains, no bunches of symbolic grapes and no cherubs to lap up the symbolic juices. The picture is presented to us undressed, just as the dancers themselves are undressed; whatever is not indispensable has been dispensed with. Both dance and dancers burst out of the frame; and in the simplifying and concentrating of the image the role of color is primary.

As much as any of the great altarpieces of the past, Matisse's *Dance* is a painting that can be seen from a great distance and still dominate the surroundings. But it differs from those altarpieces in that there is reserved for each of us a place in the very

49. Nicolas Poussin, *Bacchanalian Scene*, c. 1636–37
The National Gallery, London

XIV. Henri Matisse
The Red Studio, 1911
The Museum of Modern Art, New York

51. Henri Matisse
Bather, 1909
The Museum of Modern Art, New York

middle of the dance: it is for us, if we feel like it, to fill the gap between the outstretched hands of the two foreground figures.

Even more irresistibly are we drawn into the picture space of *The Red Studio,* 1911: the box of crayons in the foreground seems in some mysterious way to be already under our hand, and we wouldn't be surprised to see our own two familiar feet somewhere on view along the lower rim of the canvas. Color in *The Red Studio* is used to bend space in a way more radical than had been seen before in painting. Matisse takes the classic, rectangular deep space of the studio and treats it as we treat a miscellany of objects presented to us on a jeweler's tray. Certain things he picks up and puts under our noses. To others he says, ''Keep your distance!'' On the far wall, four identifiable pictures face us frontally, setting up a clear idea of the distance involved. Two identifiable statues by Matisse define, again, the space immediately in front of the far wall; but the double-A shape of the stools on which they stand is not related to the floor beneath them, any more than we can identify in the top half of the picture, the point at which the left-hand wall meets the far one. Matisse's own paintings, and his own ceramic plate in the foreground, retain their own chromatic identity. But other objects in the room have been bled of that identity and restated in terms of the glorious, uniform red which gives the picture its name. What we see is, in fact, an unbroken field of red on which certain incidents have been laid, or incised. Delectable as they are in themselves, these incidents are the captives of that one resonant, imperious, inescapable field of red. It is a crucial moment in the history of painting: color is on top, and making the most of it.

SUGGESTED READINGS

Fauvism

Crespelle, Jean-Paul. *The Fauves.*
    Greenwich, Conn., New York Graphic Society; London, Oldbourne, 1962.

Duthuit, Georges. *The Fauvist Painters.* (Documents of Modern Art ser.)
    New York, Wittenborn, 1950.

Muller, Joseph-Emile. *Fauvism.* (World of Art ser.)
    New York, Praeger, 1967.

Pierre Bonnard

Fermigier, André. *Bonnard.* (Library of Great Painters ser.)
    New York, Abrams, 1969.

André Derain

Sutton, Denys. *André Derain.*
    London, Phaidon Publishers (distributed by Doubleday), 1959.

Raoul Dufy

Werner, Alfred. *Dufy.* (Library of Great Painters ser.)
    New York, Abrams, 1970.

Henri Matisse

Barr, Alfred H., Jr. *Matisse: His Art and His Public.* Reprint.
    First publ. 1951. New York, The Museum of Modern Art, 1974.

Bowness, Alan. *Matisse and the Nude.*
    New York, The New American Library, 1968.

Guichard-Meili, Jean. *Matisse.* (World of Art ser.)
    New York, Praeger, 1967.

Lieberman, William S. *Matisse: Fifty Years of His Graphic Art.*
    New York, Braziller, 1956.

Marchiori, Giuseppe. *Matisse: The Artist and His Time.*
    New York, Reynal, 1967.

Russell, John. *The World of Matisse 1869–1954.* (Time-Life Library of Art.)
    New York, Time-Life, 1969.

Pablo Picasso

Barr, Alfred H., Jr. *Picasso: Fifty Years of His Art.* Reprint.
    First publ. 1946. New York, The Museum of Modern Art, 1974.

Cirlot, Juan-Eduardo. *Picasso: Birth of a Genius.*
    New York, Praeger, 1972.

Gilot, Françoise. *Life with Picasso.*
    New York, McGraw-Hill, 1964.

Lecaldano, Paolo. *The Complete Paintings of Picasso: Blue and Rose Periods.*
    New York, Abrams, 1972.

Los Angeles County Museum of Art. *Picasso: Blue and Rose Periods: A Catalogue Raisonné of the Paintings 1900–1906.* Daix, Pierre and Boudaille, Georges, eds.
    Greenwich, Conn., New York Graphic Society, 1967.

Penrose, Roland. *Portrait of Picasso.* 2nd rev. and enl. ed.
    First publ. 1957. New York, The Museum of Modern Art, 1971.

Rubin, William. *Picasso in the Collection of The Museum of Modern Art.*
    New York, The Museum of Modern Art, 1972.

Stein, Gertrude. *Gertrude Stein on Picasso.*
    New York, Liveright in cooperation with The Museum of Modern Art, 1970

Edouard Vuillard

Preston, Stuart. *Edouard Vuillard.* (Library of Great Painters ser.)
    New York, Abrams, 1972.

Ritchie, Andrew C. *Edouard Vuillard.* Reprint.
    First publ. 1954. New York, Arno for The Museum of Modern Art, 1969.

Russell, John. *Edouard Vuillard 1868–1940.*
    London, Thames and Hudson (distributed by New York Graphic Society), 1971.

LIST OF ILLUSTRATIONS

Dimensions: height precedes width; a third dimension, depth, is given for sculptures and constructions where revelant. Foreign titles are in English, except in cases where the title does not translate or is better known in its original form. Asterisked titles indicate works reproduced in color.

Balthus
(b. 1908)

André Derain, 1936 (fig. 17)
Oil on wood, 44⅜ x 28½ inches
The Museum of Modern Art, New York
Acquired through the Lillie P. Bliss Bequest

Bonnard, Pierre
(1867–1947)

Man and Woman, 1900 (fig. 8)
Oil on canvas, 46 x 28½ inches
Musée National d'Art Moderne, Paris

Braque, Georges
(1882–1963)

Landscape at L'Estaque, 1907 (fig. 18)
Oil on canvas, 32⅝ x 28 inches
Private collection, New York

Cézanne, Paul
(1839–1906)

Three Bathers, 1879–82 (fig. 9)
Oil on canvas, 19⅝ x 19⅝ inches
Petit Palais, Paris

The Bather, c. 1885 (fig. 5)
Oil on canvas, 50 x 38⅛ inches
The Museum of Modern Art, New York
Lillie P. Bliss Collection

David, Jacques Louis
(1748–1825)

The Oath of the Horatii, 1784 (fig. 3)
Oil on canvas, 10 feet 10 inches x 13 feet
        11½ inches
Musée du Louvre, Paris

Degas, Edgar
(1834–1917)

Harlequin, 1885 (fig. 39)
Pastel on paper, 22½ x 25½ inches
The Art Institute of Chicago
Bequest of Loula D. Lasker

The Ironers, 1882 (fig. 29)
Oil on canvas, 34¼ x 29½ inches
Norton Simon, Inc. Museum of Art, Los Angeles
The Norton Simon Foundation

Denis, Maurice
(1870–1943)

Homage to Cézanne, 1900 (fig. 22)
Oil on canvas, 70⅞ x 94½ inches
Musée National d'Art Moderne, Paris
Gift of André Gide, 1928

Derain, André
(1880–1954)

At the Suresnes Ball, 1903 (fig. 10)
Oil on canvas, 70⅞ x 57 inches
The St. Louis Art Museum

Still Life, 1904 (fig. 11)
Oil on canvas, 46 x 65½ inches
Private collection, Paris

The Golden Age, 1905 (fig. 36)
Oil on canvas, 74¼ x 69½ inches
Walter P. Chrysler, Jr., New York

The Dance, 1905–06 (fig. 50)
Oil on canvas, 73 x 90 inches
Fridart Foundation, Geneva

* *Portrait of Matisse*, 1905 (pl. VII)
Oil on canvas, 18⅛ x 13¾ inches
The Tate Gallery, London

* *Three Trees, L'Estaque*, c. 1906 (pl. VI)
Oil on canvas, 39½ x 31½ inches
Art Gallery of Ontario, Toronto
Gift of Sam and Ayala Zacks, 1970

* *London Bridge*, 1906 (pl. VIII)
Oil on canvas, 26 x 39 inches
The Museum of Modern Art, New York
Gift of Mr. and Mrs. Charles Zadok

The Old Bridge, 1910 (fig. 12)
Oil on canvas, 31⅞ x 39½ inches
National Gallery of Art, Washington, D.C.
Chester Dale Collection

Dongen, Kees van
(1877–1968)

* *Modjesko, Soprano Singer*, 1908 (pl. IX)
Oil on canvas, 39⅜ x 32 inches
The Museum of Modern Art, New York
Gift of Mr. and Mrs. Peter A Rübel

Dufy, Raoul
(1877–1953)

Beflagged Street, Le Havre, 1906 (fig. 20)
Oil on canvas, 31⅞ x 25⅞ inches
Musée National d'Art Moderne, Paris

Sailboat at Sainte-Adresse, 1912 (fig. 19)
Oil on canvas, 34⅞ x 45⅝ inches
The Museum of Modern Art, New York
Gift of Mr. and Mrs. Peter A. Rübel

Gauguin, Paul
(1848–1903)

* *Old Women of Arles*, 1888 (pl. II)
Oil on canvas, 28¾ x 36 inches
The Art Institute of Chicago
Gift of Annie Swan Coburn to the
        Mr. and Mrs. Lewis L. Coburn Memorial
        Collection

Still Life with Fruit (fig. 7)
Oil on canvas, 11¼ x 14 inches
Los Angeles County Museum of Art
Gift of Miss Merle Oberon

Gogh, Vincent van
(1853–90)

* *Bedroom at Arles*, 1888 (pl. I)
Oil on canvas, 28¾ x 36 inches
The Art Institute of Chicago
Helen Birch Bartlett Memorial Collection

Ingres, Jean Auguste Dominique
(1780–1867)

The Golden Age, 1862 (fig. 35)
Oil on paper pasted on panel, 18⅞ x 24¾ inches
Fogg Art Museum, Harvard University,
        Cambridge, Mass.
Grenville L. Winthrop Bequest

Odalisque with a Slave (fig. 33)
Oil on panel, 28⅜ x 39⅜ inches
Fogg Art Museum, Harvard University,
        Cambridge, Mass.
Grenville L. Winthrop Bequest

Manet, Edouard
(1832–83)

The Old Musician, 1862 (fig. 47)
Oil on canvas, 73¾ x 97¾ inches
National Gallery of Art, Washington, D.C.
Chester Dale Collection, 1962

Toreadors at Rest (La Posada), c. 1865 (fig. 46)
Oil on canvas, 34 x 19½ inches
Hill-Stead Museum, Farmington, Conn.

Marquet, Albert
(1875–1947)

Matisse At Work in Manguin's Studio, 1904–05
(fig. 21)
Oil on canvas, 40 x 29 inches
Musée National d'Art Moderne, Paris

The Beach at Fécamp, 1906 (fig. 16)
Oil on canvas, 20 x 24¼ inches
Musée National d'Art Moderne, Paris

Matisse, Henri
(1869–1954)

The Dessert, 1897 (fig. 1)
Oil on canvas, 39½ x 51½ inches
Private collection, Paris

Carmelina, 1903 (fig. 2)
Oil on canvas, 31½ x 25¼ inches
Museum of Fine Arts, Boston
Thompkins Collection

Portrait of Mme. Matisse with a Green Stripe, 1905
(pl. X)
Oil on canvas, 16 x 12¾ inches
The Royal Museum of Fine Arts, Copenhagen

Open Window, Collioure, 1905 (pl. XI)
Oil on canvas, 21¾ x 18⅛ inches
Mr. and Mrs. John Hay Whitney, New York

Joy of Life, 1905–06 (fig. 38)
Oil on canvas, 69½ x 95 inches
Copyright: The Barnes Foundation, Merion, Pa.

Reading, 1905–06 (fig. 23)
Oil on canvas, 29⅝ x 23⅜ inches
Private collection, New York

Self-Portrait, 1906 (fig. 43)
Oil on canvas, 22 x 18 inches
The Royal Museum of Fine Arts, Copenhagen

Bather, 1909 (fig. 51)
Oil on canvas, 36½ x 29⅛ inches
The Museum of Modern Art, New York
Gift of Abby Aldrich Rockefeller

Dance (1st version), 1909 (pl. XIII)
Oil on canvas, 8 feet 6½ inches x 12 feet
9½ inches
The Museum of Modern Art, New York
Gift of Nelson A. Rockefeller in honor of
Alfred H. Barr, Jr.

Music, 1910 (fig. 48)
Oil on canvas, 8 feet 5⅝ inches x 12 feet
9½ inches
The Hermitage, Leningrad

Jeannette IV, 1910–13 (fig. 24)
Bronze, 24⅛ inches high
The Museum of Modern Art, New York
Acquired through the Lillie P. Bliss Bequest

The Red Studio, 1911 (pl. XIV).
Oil on canvas, 71¼ x 86¼ inches
The Museum of Modern Art, New York
Mrs. Simon Guggenheim Fund

Oranges, 1912 (pl. IV)
Oil on canvas, 37 x 33⅛ inches
Estate of Pablo Picasso
Photograph: Lee Boltin for *The World of Matisse*
© 1969 Time Inc.

Picasso, Pablo
(1881–1973)

The Blue Room (La Toilette), 1901 (fig. 27)
Oil on canvas, 20 x 24½ inches
The Phillips Collection, Washington, D.C.

Self-Portrait, 1901 (fig. 25)
Oil on cardboard mounted on wood, 20¼ x 12½
inches
Mr. and Mrs. John Hay Whitney, New York

La Vie, 1903 (fig. 32)
Oil on canvas, 77⅜ x 50⅞ inches
The Cleveland Museum of Art
Gift of Hanna Fund, 1945

The Old Guitarist, 1903 (fig. 30)
Oil on panel, 47¾ x 32½ inches
The Art Institute of Chicago
Helen Birch Bartlett Memorial Collection

The Frugal Repast, 1904 (fig. 31)
Etching on zinc, 18⅜ x 14⅞ inches
The Museum of Modern Art, New York
Gift of Abby Aldrich Rockefeller

Woman Ironing, 1904 (fig. 28)
Oil on canvas, 45¾ x 28⅝ inches
The Solomon R. Guggenheim Museum, New York
Thannhauser Collection–Courtesy of the
Thannhauser Foundation

Family of Saltimbanques, 1905 (pl. XII)
Oil on canvas, 83¾ x 90⅜ inches
National Gallery of Art, Washington, D.C.
Chester Dale Collection

Two Acrobats with a Dog, 1905 (fig. 40)
Gouache on cardboard, 41½ x 29½ inches
The Museum of Modern Art, New York
Gift of Mr. and Mrs. William A. M. Burden,
New York (donor retaining life interest)

Acrobat with a Ball, 1905 (fig. 41)
Oil on canvas, 57½ x 38⅛ inches
Pushkin Museum, Moscow

Boy Leading a Horse, 1905–06 (fig. 26)
Oil on canvas, 86½ x 51¼ inches
The Museum of Modern Art, New York
Gift of William S. Paley (donor retaining life
interest)

Self-Portrait, 1906 (fig. 42)
Oil on canvas, 36¼ x 28¾ inches
Philadelphia Museum of Art
The A. E. Gallatin Collection

Horses at the Watering Place, 1906 (fig. 44)
Gouache on pulp board, 14⅞ x 23 inches
Worcester Art Museum, Worcester, Mass.
The Dial Collection

Figures in Pink (The Harem), c. 1905–06 (fig. 45)
Oil on canvas, 60¾ x 43¼ inches
The Cleveland Museum of Art
Leonard C. Hanna Jr. Collection

Poussin, Nicolas
(1593/4–1665)

Bacchanalian Scene, 1636–37 (fig. 49)
Oil on canvas, 39 x 55⅞ inches
The National Gallery, London

Puvis de Chavannes, Pierre
(1824–98)

The Sacred Grove, c. 1884 (fig. 37)
Oil on canvas, 36½ x 82⅞ inches
The Art Institute of Chicago
Potter Palmer Collection

Rouault, Georges
(1871–1958)

Samson Turning the Millstone (Ordeal of Samson),
1893 (fig. 4)
Oil on canvas, 57¾ x 44⅞ inches
Los Angeles County Museum of Art
Mr. and Mrs. George Gard de Sylva Collection

Vlaminck, Maurice
(1876–1958)

Sur le zinc, 1899 (fig. 15)
Oil on canvas, 16 x 12½ inches
Musée Calvet, Avignon, France

Houses at Chatou, 1903 (fig. 13)
Oil on canvas, 32 x 39⅝ inches
The Art Institute of Chicago
Gift of Mr. and Mrs. Maurice Culberg

The Blue House, c. 1905 (pl. III)
Oil on burlap, 21½ x 25½ inches
The Minneapolis Institute of Arts
Bequest of Putnam Dana McMillan

Self-Portrait, c. 1908 (fig. 14)
Etching, 10¼ x 7⅞ inches
The Museum of Modern Art, New York
Gift of Leon Mnuchin

Vuillard, Edouard
(1868–1940)

The Bed, 1891 (fig. 6)
Oil on canvas, 29½ x 36½ inches
Musée National d'Art Moderne, Paris

The Workshop (formerly *Interior at
L'Etang-la-Ville*), 1893 (pl. V)
Oil on millboard panel, 12½ x 14¼ inches
Smith College Museum of Art, Northampton,
Mass.

Watteau, (Jean) Antoine
(1684–1721)

Fête in the Park, c. 1720–21 (fig. 34)
Oil on canvas, 49 x 74 inches
The Wallace Collection, London